# MARY'S KITCHEN

First published 2019
by Brilliant Media, Melrose TD6 9HB

ISBN: 978 1 5272 5166 3



Layout by www.creativelink.tv

# MARY'S KITCHEN

## MY FAVOURITE RECIPES

**MARY JOAN CALDER**

# CONTENTS

## MAINS



## DESSERTS

# INTRODUCTION

My passion for cooking began at a very young age. I was fortunate to have an outstanding home economics teacher during my high school formative years and that is where my love of cooking began. I am not a formally trained chef, I am an enthusiastic self-taught home cook. I have however, over the years, enjoyed a number of cooking courses and increased my knowledge from others during my overseas travels.

In 2002, I made a very brave step of opening my own bistro and art gallery. This concept had never been done before: running a quality restaurant and displaying contemporary works of art by prominent artists. It was called the Heron Gallery & Bistro. The bistro prided itself on sourcing locally-produced ingredients whenever possible.

After many successful years in the business, I decided to officially retire (whatever that meant) and with the further experience I gained, I wanted to share my culinary knowledge with those with little or no experience in the kitchen. I wrote this book several years ago and made a decision to republish it, including a number of new recipes along with pairing each with a photograph.

I started writing my own food-related blog a few years ago, along with some occasional YouTube videos, and more currently share recipes and videos on my Facebook page "Mary's Kitchen" and Instagram. I share on a daily basis my recipes, photographs and videos through various online platforms on how to prep, cook and present dishes.

I love to cook and put a smile on people's faces, but even more I like to share my recipes and cooking knowledge with others to help them gain experience in the preparation of various foods.

I hope you get an opportunity to enjoy some of these delicious recipes and remember, I am only an email or message away should you require any hints or help.

Mary Joan Calder

LET'S STAY CONNECTED
www.marypremiercru.com

marypremiercru · Mary PremierCru · mary_premiercru · Mary's Kitchen

# SOUPS

# CULLEN SKINK

SERVES
6

MINUTES
40

DIFFICULTY
4/10

An all-time favourite. A traditional creamy Scottish fish soup made with smoked haddock, potatoes and onions.

## INGREDIENTS

**2 tbsp butter**

**1 large onion, finely chopped**

**1 large leek, finely chopped**

**1.2 litres (40fl oz) fish stock**

**1 bay leaf**

**450g (1lb) potatoes, diced**

**900ml (30fl oz) milk**

**900g (2lb) smoked undyed haddock fillet**

**300ml (10fl oz) double cream**

**3 tbsp fresh chopped parsley**

**sea salt and freshly ground black pepper**

**freshly squeezed juice of one lemon**

**fresh chopped parsley to garnish**

## METHOD

1. Heat the butter and add the chopped onion and leek. Sauté for 10 mins.
2. Add the fish stock and bay leaf, and bring to a gentle simmer. Add chopped potatoes and cook 10 mins.
3. Take a potato masher and gently mash the potatoes (not too much - you want some chunks). Add milk and at this stage, do not allow to boil.
4. Now add the whole fish fillets and continue to heat until you can flake the fish right in the pot. Large flakes are best.
5. Once you have flaked fish slowly add cream, again, do not boil.
6. Add the chopped parsley and season as necessary with sea salt and freshly ground pepper.
7. Add lemon juice to taste to give a wee zing. If the soup is too thick add a little more of the fish stock to thin out a bit.
8. Serve soup topped with parsley.

## MARY'S TIP

Don't skimp on the fish then you will have a meal in itself.

# POTATO & LEEK

SERVES
6

MINUTES
50

DIFFICULTY
1/10

I prefer not to purée this soup so I use a good quality waxy potato – you want a potato that holds its shape and doesn't fall apart while cooking.

## INGREDIENTS

**75g (3oz) butter (grass-fed if possible)**

**1 tbsp vegetable oil**

**1 large onion, chopped**

**3 large leeks, sliced thinly, washed well and drained**

**5 large potatoes, peeled and cubed**

**sea salt and pepper**

**1 tbsp mixed dried herbs**

**1.2 litres (40fl oz) vegetable stock**

**300ml (10fl oz) milk**

**chopped chives to garnish**

## METHOD

1. Melt the butter and oil over a low heat and add the onion, leeks and potatoes. Sprinkle with sea salt, pepper and the mixed herbs.
2. Keep the heat very low and allow the vegetables to sweat for 15 minutes in the butter and oil.
3. Add the stock and bring to a boil. Turn the heat down to a simmer and cook for 30 minutes or until vegetables are tender.
4. Add the milk and simmer for a further 5 minutes. You can purée but I prefer to serve this soup chunky.
5. Top with chopped chives.

MARY'S TIP

Add more stock for desired consistency.

# CREAM OF CAULIFLOWER

SERVES 6

MINUTES 40

DIFFICULTY 1/10

The addition of sherry and mustard takes this bland vegetable into a new realm.

## INGREDIENTS

**50g (2oz) butter**

**1 large onion, finely chopped**

**2 garlic cloves, peeled and chopped**

**1 heaped tsp powdered mustard**

**140ml (5fl oz) medium to dry sherry**

**2 medium cauliflowers, trimmed and broken into florets**

**1.2 litres (40fl oz) vegetable stock**

**salt and pepper**

**freshly chopped parsley or chives to garnish**

## METHOD

1. Melt the butter in large soup pot and sauté the onion until golden.
2. Add garlic, mustard powder, 120ml (4fl oz) of the sherry, and the cauliflower florets. Mix well and cook over a low heat for 10 minutes.
3. Add vegetable stock and simmer for 20-30 minutes or until cauliflower is tender.
4. Purée the soup until a smooth consistency is reached. Add a little more vegetable stock if soup is too thick.
5. Season with salt and pepper to taste, add remaining sherry then serve topped with some chopped parsley and chives.

## MARY'S TIP

A lot of supermarkets now sell cauliflower florets already prepared – a nice time saver.

# RUSTIC FRENCH LENTIL

SERVES
6

MINUTES
80

DIFFICULTY
2/10

A hearty winter warmer. Was always a popular dish with the French farming community.

## INGREDIENTS

**1 tbsp olive oil**

**2 medium onions, finely chopped**

**8 rashers of smoked back bacon, finely chopped**

**2 carrots, peeled and finely chopped**

**2 garlic cloves, peeled and chopped**

**2 celery sticks, thinly sliced**

**225g (8oz) red lentils, washed and drained**

**1.8 litres (60fl oz) vegetable stock**

**1 x 400g tin chopped tomatoes**

**salt and pepper**

**3 tbsp freshly chopped parsley**

## METHOD

1 Heat the oil in a large pot and sauté the onions and bacon together over a gentle heat.

2 Add the carrots, garlic and celery, and allow to cook for 5 minutes.

3 Add the lentils, vegetable stock, tomatoes, salt and pepper. Bring to a boil, then cover and turn down to simmer. Cook for about one hour, stirring occasionally (if too thick add some more stock).

4 Check seasoning. Just before serving stir in the chopped parsley.

MARY'S TIP

As the French did – lovely with a crusty baguette.

# CARROT & ORANGE

SERVES
6

MINUTES
45

DIFFICULTY
2/10

The addition of orange rind and juice in this soup brings out the sweet flavour of the carrots.

## INGREDIENTS

**1 tbsp vegetable oil**

**1 tbsp butter**

**1 large onion, chopped**

**900g (2lb) carrots, peeled and sliced**

**grated rind of one orange**

**300ml (10fl oz) orange juice**

**2 garlic cloves, crushed**

**sea salt and freshly ground pepper**

**1.2 litres (40fl oz) vegetable stock**

**cream and grated orange rind to garnish**

## METHOD

1 Heat the oil and butter, and sauté the chopped onion.

2 Add the carrots, orange rind and juice along with garlic, sea salt and freshly ground pepper. Sweat over a gentle heat for 20 minutes.

3 Add the stock and bring to the boil, then turn down to simmer.

4 Once the carrots are tender, purée the soup. If the soup is too thick add some more orange juice or vegetable stock to reach the desired thickness. Check seasoning.

5 Garnish - a swirl of cream (if desired) and freshly grated orange rind.

### MARY'S TIP

Always use the freshest carrots for the sweetest flavour – organic are by far the best.

# CARROT & CARAWAY

Try and use fresh local farm-grown organic carrots when possible. They are deliciously sweet and make a huge difference to flavour.

SERVES
6

MINUTES
90

DIFFICULTY
3/10

## INGREDIENTS

**3 tbsp vegetable oil or 1/2 oil, 1/2 butter**

**1 large Spanish onion, chopped**

**900g (2lb) organic carrots, peeled and chopped**

**1 heaped tbsp caraway seeds**

**175ml (6fl oz) dry sherry**

**1.2 litres (40fl oz) vegetable stock**

**sea salt and pepper to taste**

**freshly chopped parsley and roasted caraway seeds to garnish**

## METHOD

1 Heat the oil (or melt butter & oil) in a large soup pot. Add the onion and sauté gently.

2 Add the carrots, caraway seeds and sherry. Place a piece of damp greaseproof paper between the pot and lid and let these ingredients sweat for a good hour on the lowest heat. Stir occasionally.

3 Add your vegetable stock and cook for another half-hour.

4 Once the carrots are tender, use your hand blender and blend the soup until you have a nice smooth consistency. Add a little more stock if the soup appears to be too thick.

5 Season to taste then garnish with roasted caraway seeds and freshly chopped parsley. Serve with some warm crusty bread.

MARY'S TIP

*If you don't have sherry, a dry white wine is a good substitute.*

# CELERY, FENNEL & STILTON

SERVES
6

MINUTES
70

DIFFICULTY
3/10

An excellent balance of flavours from the subtle taste of celery, to the more punchy taste of stilton and rounded off with the anise flavour of fennel.

## INGREDIENTS

**3 tbsp vegetable oil**

**1 large onion, chopped**

**3 heads of celery, chopped**

**1 bulb of fennel, chopped**

**1 tsp fennel seeds**

**1.2 litres (40fl oz) vegetable stock**

**sea salt and freshly ground pepper to taste**

**225g (8oz) Stilton cheese or any other kind of blue cheese, chopped**

**140ml (5fl oz) cream**

**finely chopped chives and flaked crumbs of blue cheese to garnish**

## METHOD

1. Heat the oil and sauté the onion in a large soup pot. Add chopped celery, fennel and fennel seeds. Sauté for a further 15 minutes, stirring occasionally.
2. Add the stock and cook for 30-40 minutes or until celery and fennel are tender.
3. Add sea salt and pepper to taste. Using a hand blender, purée the soup until a smooth consistency has been reached.
4. Add the Stilton cheese and allow to melt through soup. Stir in cream and garnish with chives and flaked crumbs of blue cheese.

MARY'S TIP

*Use any type of blue cheese you enjoy with this soup.*

# FRENCH ONION AU GRATIN

SERVES
4

MINUTES
45

DIFFICULTY
4/10

This is one of my personal all-time favourites and the way it should be made. Avoid any short cuts.

## INGREDIENTS

**6 medium onions, thinly sliced**

**2.5 tbsp of olive oil**

**1.5 tbsp of butter**

**110ml (4fl oz) dry sherry**

**2 tbsp plain flour**

**1.5 litres (50fl oz) beef stock**

**240ml (8fl oz) white wine**

**1 heaped tbsp chopped fresh thyme**

**1 bay leaf**

**1 heaped tbsp chopped fresh chervil or parsley**

**sea salt and cracked black pepper to taste**

**350g (12oz) Gruyère cheese, grated**

**225g (8oz) Emmental cheese, grated**

**French bread sliced to 2cm thickness and toasted**

## METHOD

1 Separate the onion rings and sauté in oil and butter over a low heat. Stir until golden brown.

2 Add the sherry and simmer for 15 mins.

3 Sprinkle with plain flour and stir until blended into onions. Gradually add beef stock and white wine.

4 Add herbs and seasoning and stir until the soup begins to boil. Lower heat and simmer for 20 mins.

5 In each bowl put 1 tbsp of Gruyère and 1 tbsp of Emmental. Add soup on top of cheese.

6 Place one slice of toasted French bread on top of soup, add more cheese on top of bread and put under grill until the cheese browns.

MARY'S TIP

When you add the sherry – caramelising the onions further deepens the flavour.

# DETOX CABBAGE

SERVES
8

MINUTES
90

DIFFICULTY
1/10

This is a dieter's delight. A substantial soup that is great for detoxing.

## INGREDIENTS

**1.5 litres (50fl oz) vegetable stock**

**225g (8oz) carrots, shredded**

**150g (5oz) celery, chopped**

**2 potatoes, peeled and cubed**

**1 large onion, chopped**

**1 x 400g tin chopped tomatoes**

**2 tsp salt**

**1 bay leaf**

**8 whole peppercorns**

**1 whole cabbage (Savoy or white), shredded**

**juice from 1 lemon**

## METHOD

1. Combine the vegetable stock, carrots, celery, potatoes, onion, tomatoes, salt, bay leaf and peppercorns. Bring to a boil and then turn down to simmer for one hour.
2. Add the shredded cabbage and lemon juice, and simmer for another 30 minutes.

MARY'S TIP

This soup lends itself to adding any type of vegetable you wish.

# CREAM OF MUSHROOM & BRANDY

SERVES
4

MINUTES
60

DIFFICULTY
1/10

Any type of mushroom can be used for this soup, but on a cost basis I have opted for chestnut mushrooms.

## INGREDIENTS

**50g (2oz) butter**

**1 large onion, chopped**

**2 garlic cloves, chopped**

**450g (1lb) chestnut mushrooms, chopped**

**150ml (5fl oz) brandy**

**1 tsp dried tarragon**

**900ml (30fl oz) vegetable stock**

**sea salt and pepper**

**450ml (15fl oz) milk**

**150ml (5fl oz) fresh double cream**

**finely chopped parsley, cream, and sliced mushroom to garnish**

## METHOD

1. Melt the butter in large pot. Sauté the onion and garlic in butter.
2. Add the mushrooms to the onions and continue to sauté until the mushrooms soften.
3. Add the brandy and the tarragon and allow to sweat for 10 minutes.
4. Add the stock, sea salt and pepper. Bring to a boil and turn down to a simmer for 30 minutes.
5. Just before serving slowly add the milk and cream. Purée the soup. Check seasoning.
6. To serve garnish with a swirl of cream, slices of freshly sliced mushroom and chopped parsley.

## MARY'S TIP

If you don't have brandy to hand, sherry is a good alternative.

# CREAM OF SPINACH

SERVES 6

MINUTES 30

DIFFICULTY 1/10

One of my firm favourites as it is simple and easy to prepare. Spinach has a lovely peppery taste and it's best to use organic baby leaf spinach if possible.

## INGREDIENTS

**3 tbsp coconut or avocado oil**

**2 large onions, chopped**

**3 packs of organic spinach, washed and drained**

**sea salt and freshly ground pepper**

**pinch of freshly grated nutmeg**

**1.2 litres (40fl oz) vegetable stock**

**300ml (10fl oz) double cream**

**extra cream to serve**

## METHOD

1. Heat the oil and sauté the chopped onion.
2. Add the spinach, sea salt and freshly ground pepper and a pinch of grated nutmeg. Cover the pot and allow to sweat down for 5 minutes.
3. Add the vegetable stock. Cook on a low heat for 20 minutes then slowly add cream.
4. Purée the soup and season as necessary.
5. To serve add a swirl of cream on top of each bowl before serving.

MARY'S TIP

While wilting the spinach – keep heat very low as you do not want to discolour the leaves.

# CURRIED PARSNIP & APPLE

SERVES
6

MINUTES
40

DIFFICULTY
1/10

Parsnips may be underrated vegetables but don't be fooled. They are high in fibre, vitamins and minerals, in particular vitamins C & K and folate (which is a superfood for pregnant women).

## INGREDIENTS

**50g (2oz) butter**

**1 large onion, chopped**

**1 heaped tbsp curry powder**

**900g (2lb) parsnips, peeled and chopped**

**1 large cooking apple**

**1.2 litres (40 fl oz) vegetable stock**

**sea salt and cracked black pepper**

**2 tbsp freshly chopped coriander and thin slices of apple to garnish**

## METHOD

1. In a large pot melt the butter, add the chopped onion and sauté on a low heat.
2. Add the curry powder, parsnips and apple stirring well.
3. Next add the vegetable stock, sea salt and pepper. Cook on a low heat for 30 minutes or until parsnips are softened.
4. Purée. Garnish with thin slices of apple and fresh coriander.

MARY'S TIP
Using a veg peeler, I like to take some thin slices of parsnip and crisp up in coconut oil to use as a garnish.

# CHUNKY TOMATO & BASIL

SERVES
6

MINUTES
45

DIFFICULTY
1/10

Tomatoes and fresh basil are a match made in heaven. The two flavours pair together in so many different dishes.

## INGREDIENTS

**2 tbsp olive oil**

**1 large onion, chopped**

**1/2 tube tomato paste**

**4 x 400g tins chopped tomatoes**

**900ml (30fl oz) vegetable stock**

**3 tbsp fresh chopped basil**

**1 tbsp dried mixed herbs**

**sea salt and black cracked pepper**

**fresh chopped basil and cream to serve**

## METHOD

1. Sauté the chopped onion in olive oil in a large pot. Add the tomato paste and stir into the onion for 1 minute.
2. Add the tinned tomatoes and the vegetable stock. Bring to the boil.
3. Turn down to a simmer and add 3 tablespoons of chopped fresh basil, the mixed herbs, salt and pepper. Simmer for 30 minutes.
4. Purée gently (you still want some consistency in this soup). To serve garnish with fresh chopped basil and a swirl of cream.

MARY'S TIP

This soup can be made with fresh tomatoes but they need to be peeled first. To release peel quickly, pour boiling water over tomatoes, leave for 5 minutes then drain, and peel will come off with ease.

# ROASTED RED PEPPER & ORANGE

SERVES
6

MINUTES
75

DIFFICULTY
6/10

This colourful soup has a depth of flavour and is truly delicious and warming on a cold autumn day.

## INGREDIENTS

**8 large red peppers, chopped in half and seeded**

**6 tbsp olive oil**

**2 large onions, chopped**

**120ml (4fl oz) dry sherry**

**1.2 litres (40fl oz) vegetable stock**

**150ml (5fl oz) orange juice**

**grated rind of one orange**

**1 tbsp fresh chopped coriander**

**chopped coriander and orange rind to garnish**

## METHOD

1. Preheat the oven to 200C/400F/gas mark 6.
2. Place the red peppers on a baking tray skin upwards and sprinkle with olive oil. Bake for 15–20 minutes or until the skins are blackened.
3. Remove from the oven and place in a plastic bag for 5 minutes. This will assist in the easy removal of the outer skins.
4. Remove the skin from the red peppers and chop into large pieces.
5. Heat the remaining olive oil in a pan and sauté the chopped onions. Add the roasted red peppers and sherry. Sweat for 15 minutes.
6. Add the stock, orange juice and rind, and cook for 30 minutes over a gentle heat.
7. Add the fresh coriander. Purée the soup. Add a little more orange juice or stock to obtain the desired consistency.
8. Garnish with chopped fresh coriander and orange rind.

MARY'S TIP

To save time you can buy roasted peppers, ready-prepared in a jar.

# ROASTED BUTTERNUT SQUASH

SERVES
6

MINUTES
75

DIFFICULTY
3/10

A great source of vitamins A and C, butternut squash is at its best in the U.K. from September to December.

## INGREDIENTS

**1 large butternut squash**

**2 tbsp olive oil**

**2 tbsp coconut oil**

**2 onions, chopped**

**3 garlic cloves, chopped**

**1 red chilli, deseeded and chopped**

**1 heaped tsp ground cumin**

**710ml (24fl oz) vegetable stock**

**120ml (4fl oz) cream**

## METHOD

1 Preheat the oven to 180C/350F/gas mark 4.

2 Cut the butternut squash in half and scoop the seeds out. Coat the flesh in olive oil and place face down on baking sheet. Bake for 45 minutes until the squash is tender.

3 In a large pan heat the coconut oil, and sauté the onions, garlic, chilli and cumin for a few minutes.

4 Once the butternut squash is soft and tender (test with a fork) – scoop out the flesh and add to the pan, pour in the vegetable stock then add the cream. Cook on a low heat for 30 minutes.

5 Use a handheld blender to purée the soup in the pan or transfer the soup to a food processor.

MARY'S TIP

For a twist on this recipe, you can add 2 roasted sweet potatoes and a can of coconut milk.

# STARTERS

# BAKED GOAT'S CHEESE WITH TOMATO, TARRAGON & CHORIZO

SERVES
4

MINUTES
20

DIFFICULTY
1/10

This makes a great starter for vegetarians – just omit chorizo.

## INGREDIENTS

**4 tomatoes, sliced**

**225g (8oz) goat's cheese, cut in to 8 slices**

**20 thin slices of chorizo (Spanish sausage)**

**sprinkling of olive oil**

**sprinkling of tarragon leaves (fresh if possible)**

**squeeze of lemon juice**

**French bread**

## METHOD

1. You will need 4 oval eared dishes.
2. Slice the tomatoes thinly and place them around the oval eared dishes, place one slice in centre of each dish.
3. Place two slices of goat's cheese in the centre of each dish then layer 5 slices of chorizo sausage over the tomatoes. Sprinkle each dish with olive oil and tarragon leaves, then add squeeze of lemon juice.
4. Bake in a preheated oven 200C/400F/gas mark 6 for 15 minutes.
5. Serve with slices of fresh French bread.

MARY'S TIP

Use a goat's cheese that does not have rind on it so it melts nicely into the tomatoes.

# CHICKEN LIVER PÂTÉ AU COGNAC

SERVES 6

MINUTES 30

DIFFICULTY 3/10

A good pâté is a dish that people never lose interest in. This recipe's subtle flavours of brandy and herbs make it a star performer at any dinner party.

## INGREDIENTS

**225g (8oz) butter (grass-fed if possible)**

**225g (8oz) chicken livers**

**3 tbsp brandy**

**2 tsp English mustard**

**2 tsp fresh thyme (or 1 tsp dried)**

**1 tsp fresh sage (or 1 tsp dried)**

**3 garlic cloves, peeled and crushed**

**sea salt and fresh ground pepper**

## METHOD

1. In a heavy-based frying pan melt 25g (1oz) of butter. Fry the chicken livers over medium heat for 5 minutes, stirring frequently.
2. Remove from pan and transfer to a food processor. Melt 150g (5oz) of butter and add to blender.
3. Pour the brandy onto the juices left in the frying pan and then pour over liver.
4. Add the mustard, thyme, sage, garlic, sea salt and pepper. Blend on high until you have a velvety creamy pâté.
5. Place the pâté in a ceramic dish and melt the remaining butter and pour over top of pâté. Leave to cool.
6. Cover and place in the fridge for at least 3 hours.
7. Serve with toast or oatcakes or a small mixed leaf salad and a spoonful of redcurrant jelly.

MARY'S TIP

The additional melted butter on top keeps the pâté from discolouring.

# CARAMELISED RED ONION TARTLETS WITH GOAT'S CHEESE

SERVES
8

MINUTES
90

DIFFICULTY
8/10

These are so pretty – excellent for ladies who do lunch – serve one each with a mixed leaf salad.

*You will need 8 mini flan tins (base diameter 10cm [4"]) with removable bases.*

## INGREDIENTS

### PASTRY

**75g (3oz) butter**
**175g (6oz) plain flour**
**50g (2oz) grated parmesan cheese**
**half tsp mustard powder**
**half tsp cayenne pepper**
**1 egg, beaten**

### FILLING

**25g (1oz) butter (grass-fed if possible) & a splash of olive oil**
**900g (2lb) red onions, peeled and finely chopped**
**6 tbsp balsamic vinegar**
**1 tbsp chopped fresh sage, plus 8 sage leaves for topping**
**sea salt and freshly milled black pepper**
**225g (8oz) goat's cheese, cut into 8 rounds**
**1 tbsp olive oil**
**cayenne pepper**

## METHOD

### PASTRY

1 Preheat the oven to 180C/350F/gas mark 4.

2 Rub butter into flour, add cheese, mustard, cayenne pepper and just enough cold water to make dough. Allow the dough to rest in fridge for 30 minutes.

3 Roll pastry out thinly and cut out 8 rounds. Grease and line the flan tins.

4 Fork them all over and brush with beaten egg, place onto a baking sheet. Cook for 15-20 minutes, then allow to cool.

### FILLING

1 Melt the butter and olive oil in a heavy-based saucepan. Stir in the onions, balsamic vinegar and chopped sage. Season with sea salt and pepper and cook very gently without a lid for 30 minutes. Stir regularly until the excess liquid has evaporated.

2 Spoon equal amounts of the onion mixture into each case. Add the goat's cheese on top and a sage leaf that has been dipped in a little olive oil.

3 Sprinkle with cayenne pepper and bake for 20 minutes.

## MARY'S TIP

Don't worry if you do not have individual pie dishes, just use a shallow 20cm (8") flan dish. If you do this – double up the ingredients in the recipe.

# MOULES MARINIÈRE

SERVES
4

MINUTES
60

DIFFICULTY
6/10

Always use the freshest mussels you can find. If possible, buy rope mussels as you will find these almost grit-free.

**Soak the mussels for 30 minutes in lightly salted water then rinse under cold running water, lightly scrub and de-beard using a small sharp knife.**

**Discard any broken mussels or open mussels that do not shut when tapped firmly with the back of a knife. This indicates they are dead and could cause severe food poisoning if eaten. Rinse the mussels again.**

## INGREDIENTS

**4 tbsp olive oil**

**1 garlic clove, finely chopped**

**2 x 400g tins chopped tomatoes**

**350ml (12fl oz) white wine**

**rind and juice of 1 lemon**

**2 tbsp finely chopped fresh parsley**

**2.25kg (5 lb) mussels**

**2 tbsp freshly chopped coriander**

**sea salt and pepper**

**fresh parsley to garnish**

## METHOD

1 Heat the oil in large stockpot over a medium heat. Add the garlic and sauté for about 3 minutes to flavour the oil.

2 Add the tomatoes, wine, lemon rind and juice along with parsley. Bring to the boil and then lower heat. Cover and simmer for 5 minutes.

3 Add the mussels, cover and simmer for 5-8 minutes, shaking the pan regularly, until they are open.

4 Finally, sprinkle in the chopped coriander and season with salt and pepper. Use a slotted spoon and transfer them to serving bowls. Discard any mussels that did not open during cooking.

5 Ladle the sauce over the mussels and sprinkle with extra fresh parsley. Serve at once with plenty of fresh French bread to mop up the delicious juices.

## MARY'S TIP

Always have an extra bowl either in the middle of the table or beside each person to put discarded shells into.

# MUSHROOMS AU GRATIN

SERVES
4

MINUTES
30

DIFFICULTY
4/10

A rich and delicious starter for mushroom lovers – ultimate comfort food.

## INGREDIENTS

**50g (2oz) butter (grass-fed if possible)**

**1 onion, finely chopped**

**2 garlic cloves, peeled and finely chopped**

**150ml (5fl oz) white wine**

**1 tsp lemon juice**

**1 tsp dried mixed herbs**

**1 tsp dried tarragon**

**sea salt and pepper**

**2 packs white or chestnut mushrooms, sliced**

**300ml (10fl oz) double cream**

**4 tbsp wholemeal breadcrumbs (gluten free if desired)**

**110g (4oz) grated parmesan cheese**

## METHOD

1. Melt the butter in a large frying pan. Add the onions and garlic and sauté gently.
2. Add the white wine, lemon juice, mixed herbs and tarragon. Add a pinch of sea salt, pepper and sliced mushrooms. Sauté gently for 15 minutes.
3. Add the cream and cook gently for a further 5 minutes.
4. Divide equally into 4 oval eared dishes.
5. Mix the breadcrumbs and grated parmesan together. Sprinkle on top and place under a hot grill until the topping browns and the mushrooms are bubbling.

## MARY'S TIP

When adding cream you can add a 1/4 tsp of English mustard for extra flavour.

# PORTOBELLO MUSHROOMS, TOMATOES & GOAT'S CHEESE

SERVES
4

MINUTES
30

DIFFICULTY
2/10

This is a tasty vegetarian dish that can be served as a starter for 4 people or a light lunch for 2.

## INGREDIENTS

**4 Portobello mushrooms**

**20 cherry tomatoes, chopped**

**1 garlic clove, finely chopped**

**olive oil**

**squeeze of lemon juice**

**sea salt and pepper**

**a sprinkle of dried tarragon**

**225g (8oz) goat's cheese**

**4 slices of thinly sliced lemon**

## METHOD

1. Remove the middle stalk from the mushrooms.
2. Combine the chopped cherry tomatoes, finely chopped garlic, a dash of olive oil, lemon juice, sea salt and pepper.
3. Evenly fill the mushroom cups with the mixture. Sprinkle some tarragon on top of the tomatoes, then finish off by adding 50g (2oz) goat's cheese to each mushroom top.
4. Add another dash of olive oil to each. Top each with a slice of lemon.
5. Bake in a preheated oven 180C/350F/gas mark 4 for 20 minutes.

MARY'S TIP

If you can find lemon pepper in the supermarket, add a sprinkle to each one.

# SMOKED MACKEREL PÂTÉ

SERVES
6-8

MINUTES
10

DIFFICULTY
1/10

A recipe you will make over and over again. Store bought smoked mackerel is fine to use for this dish but if you can get fresh smoked mackerel it makes a big difference.

## INGREDIENTS

**4 single smoked mackerel fillets**

**2 single peppered smoked mackerel fillets**

**1 green chilli, deseeded and chopped**

**1 red chilli, deseeded and chopped**

**4 tbsp fresh coriander leaves**

**1 small red onion, chopped**

**grated rind of one lime and one lemon**

**juice of one lime & one lemon**

**225g (8oz) cream cheese**

**1 garlic clove (if desired)**

**fresh chopped parsley to garnish**

## METHOD

1. Remove the skin from the mackerel fillets and discard along with any tiny bones.
2. Break the fish up into small pieces and place in a food processor, along with all the other ingredients.
3. Blend on high until you end up with a smooth pâté.
4. Spoon the mixture into suitable dish and sprinkle with chopped parsley.
5. Allow to cool in the fridge for at least two hours.
6. Serve with oatcakes and a small mixed salad.

**MARY'S TIP**

If I want a bigger kick, I use all peppered mackerel.

# SPICY BARBECUED CHICKEN WINGS

SERVES
4-6

MINUTES
60

DIFFICULTY
3/10

A banging party dish – no napkins required, they are finger licking good.

## INGREDIENTS

**900g (2lb) chicken wings, tips removed and centre joint cut in half (creating two pieces of wing)**

### MARINADE

**240ml (8fl oz) tomato ketchup**

**2 tbsp olive oil**

**1 heaped tsp ground cumin**

**1 red chilli, deseeded and chopped**

**1 green chilli, deseeded and chopped**

**2 garlic cloves, peeled and crushed**

**1 tsp dark brown muscovado sugar**

**1 tbsp Worcester sauce**

**1 tbsp lemon juice**

**55ml (2fl oz) water**

**sea salt and pepper to taste**

## METHOD

1 Mix all the marinade ingredients, coat each wing piece and leave to marinate for 2 hours.

2 Preheat the oven to 200C/400F/gas mark 6.

3 Place foil on the bottom of a large baking tray and line with the wings. Try not to overlap. Cook for 30 - 40 minutes, turning halfway through cooking.

MARY'S TIP

Serve with a small mixed leaf salad as an appetiser.

# THAI FISH CAKES

SERVES
6

MINUTES
75

DIFFICULTY
4/10

Thai fish cakes are delightful served with sweet chilli dipping sauce and/or peanut sauce – see recipes on page 54.

## INGREDIENTS

**450g (1lb) haddock or cod fillet**

**3 spring onions, finely chopped**

**1 red chilli, deseeded and finely chopped**

**1 tbsp ginger root, finely chopped**

**1 clove of garlic, chopped**

**grated rind of two limes**

**juice of two limes**

**3 heaped tbsp fresh coriander, chopped**

**3 tbsp sesame oil**

## METHOD

1 Put all the ingredients (except the sesame oil) in a food processor and blend until smooth. Divide the mixture into 8–12 equal amounts, then shape into 8–12 small/medium sized fish cakes. Put on a plate, cover and chill for one hour.

2 Heat oil in a shallow non-stick frying pan and cook fish cakes over a medium heat, 3 minutes per side.

3 Serve with wedges of lime, mixed leaf salad and sweet chilli dipping sauce (see recipe on page 54) .

MARY'S TIP

Very nice as a light lunch served with a mixed salad.

# SWEET CHILLI DIP

SERVES 4

MINUTES 5

DIFFICULTY 1/10

## INGREDIENTS

**1 tbsp fresh ginger, finely chopped**

**1 red chilli, deseeded and finely chopped (leave seeds in if you prefer a hotter sauce)**

**2 tbsp light brown muscovado sugar**

**1 tbsp light soy sauce**

**2 tbsp dry sherry**

## METHOD

1 Place all the ingredients in a food processor and blend until smooth.

# PEANUT DIP

SERVES 4

MINUTES 5

DIFFICULTY 1/10

## INGREDIENTS

**1 small red chilli, deseeded and finely chopped**

**1 tbsp light soy sauce**

**1 tbsp lime juice**

**1 tbsp light brown muscovado sugar**

**3 tbsp 100% palm oil-free chunky peanut butter**

**4 tbsp coconut milk**

## METHOD

1 Place all the ingredients into a small saucepan and heat gently, stirring constantly, until well blended.

# MANGO SALSA

SERVES
6

MINUTES
15

DIFFICULTY
2/10

This is delicious served with scrambled eggs, on top of burgers, baked potatoes or simply eaten with tortilla chips.

## INGREDIENTS

**12 medium vine tomatoes, chopped**

**2 red onions, finely chopped**

**1 red chilli, deseeded and chopped**

**1 green chilli, deseeded and chopped**

**3 tbsp fresh coriander**

**3 tbsp fresh parsley**

**1 fresh mango, chopped**

**3 garlic cloves, finely chopped**

**grated rind of 2 limes**

**juice of 2 limes**

**1 tsp sea salt**

**generous turn of freshly milled pepper**

## METHOD

1. Place all the ingredients in a food processor and pulse until all ingredients are finely chopped.

MARY'S TIP

Some like it HOT! (If you do, do not deseed the chillies.)

# MAINS

# SPICY TURKEY MEATBALLS WITH CHILLI & RED PEPPER SAUCE

SERVES
4

MINUTES
75

DIFFICULTY
4/10

Ground turkey (minced turkey) has become a firm favourite in our home. Try swapping ground beef (minced beef) for turkey – you will get a pleasant surprise and it's an exceedingly healthy option.

## INGREDIENTS

### MEATBALLS

**450g (1lb) lean ground turkey (minced turkey)**
**1 red chilli, chopped**
**1 egg, beaten**
**1.5 slices of gluten free or wholemeal bread made into crumbs (use your hand-held blender to crumb bread)**
**1 onion, chopped**
**1 tsp thyme (dried or fresh)**
**2 garlic cloves, chopped**
**1 tsp mixed herbs (dried or fresh)**
**1 tbsp Worcester sauce**
**50g (2oz) parmesan, grated**
**sea salt and pepper**
**olive oil, to fry**

### SAUCE

**1 tbsp olive oil**
**1 onion, chopped**
**2 sweet red peppers (long pointed variety), chopped**
**1 red chilli, chopped**
**1 garlic clove, chopped**
**1 x 400g tin tomatoes**
**300ml (10fl oz) water**

## METHOD

### MEATBALLS

1. Mix all the ingredients together and divide into 12–16 balls.
2. Heat a tbsp of olive oil in a non-stick frying pan and cook the meatballs until brown all over. Remove from the pan and set aside resting on paper towel.

### SAUCE

1. Add 1 more tbsp olive oil to same pan. Add onion, peppers, chilli and garlic. Cook for 5 minutes or until everything is soft.
2. Add tomatoes and water. Cook on medium heat for 15–20 minutes.
3. Take off heat and allow to cool slightly. Put in blender and blend until smooth.
4. Return sauce to same pan and add meatballs. Simmer for a further 30 minutes.

## MARY'S TIP

You can easily make this recipe a day before and allow meatballs to infuse with the sauce. Serve over your favourite pasta or for a healthier option – spiralised courgette. Top with grated parmesan.

# THAI-SPICED CORIANDER CHICKEN

SERVES
4

MINUTES
80

DIFFICULTY
2/10

These chicken breasts are packed with powerful, zesty flavours and are best accompanied by simple plain long grain rice and a cucumber salad.

## INGREDIENTS

**4 boneless, skinless chicken breasts**

**4 garlic cloves, peeled**

**1 green chilli, whole**

**2cm (0.75") fresh ginger root, peeled**

**4 tbsp fresh coriander leaves, chopped**

**rind of 1 lime, finely grated**

**3 tbsp lime juice**

**2 tbsp light soy sauce**

**1 tbsp coconut sugar**

**175ml (6fl oz) coconut milk**

## METHOD

1. Using a sharp knife, cut 3 deep slashes into each breast. Place the breasts in a single layer in a non-metallic dish.
2. Put the garlic, green chilli, ginger, coriander, lime rind and juice, soy sauce, coconut sugar and coconut milk in a mini blender or food processor and purée.
3. Spread the purée over both sides of the chicken, cover the dish with clingfilm and leave to marinate in fridge for one hour (or longer).
4. Preheat the oven to 180C/350F/gas mark 4.
5. Remove the chicken from marinade, draining off any excess and place in a baking pan. Bake in the oven for 20 minutes or until evenly cooked.
6. Meanwhile, place the remaining marinade in a saucepan and bring to the boil. Lower the heat and simmer for several minutes. At this stage you can add a drop more coconut milk to thin it out if required.
7. Spoon over the chicken breasts.

MARY'S TIP
Serve with saffron, butter or basmati rice and cucumber salad.

# SPINACH, FETA CHEESE & CHERRY TOMATO TART

SERVES
6

MINUTES
45

DIFFICULTY
3/10

A lovely colourful tart that makes an excellent light supper.

*You will need one 20cm (8") prepared pastry case.*
*See page 66 for recipe.*

## INGREDIENTS

**50g (2oz) butter (grass-fed if possible)**

**1 large onion, chopped**

**1 bag pre-washed baby spinach**

**sea salt and pepper**

**4 large eggs**

**300ml (10fl oz) double cream or crème fraîche**

**110g (4oz) feta cheese, crumbled**

**10 cherry tomatoes, halved**

## METHOD

1 Preheat the oven to 190C/375F/gas mark 5.

2 Melt the butter in large deep frying pan with lid. Add the chopped onion and sauté gently. Add the spinach, cover pan, and allow to sweat for 5 minutes. Season with sea salt and pepper.

3 Drain off any excess butter. Place the spinach mixture in your prepared pastry case and spread evenly over the bottom of the case.

4 In a bowl beat the eggs and double cream together, season to taste, then pour the mixture over the spinach.

5 Crumble feta cheese over top of the mixture and strategically place cherry tomatoes carefully in and around cheese.

6 Place on baking tray and bake for 35 minutes or until firm to the touch.

MARY'S TIP

Buy the best quality feta and cherry tomatoes you can.

# SHORTCRUST PASTRY (SAVOURY OR SWEET)

SERVES
16

MINUTES
90

DIFFICULTY
4/10

This is a very easy method of making shortcrust pastry by using a food processor. You can also do by hand but it is laborious and a bit messy.

*This recipe makes 2 x 20cm (8") pastry cases.*

## INGREDIENTS

**225g (8oz) plain flour**

**60g (2.5oz) butter**

**60g (2.5oz) margarine**

**1 egg**

**Cold water as required**

**(for a sweet version of this pastry add 1 tbsp of caster sugar)**

## METHOD

1. Add the first 3 ingredients to your food processor and mix at a high speed until mixture is crumbly. Add the egg and continue to mix. Slowly add cold water until mixture forms a clump. Do not add too much water as dough will become sticky. Take out of processor, and wrap in cling film and chill for one hour in fridge.

2. Divide into 2 equal portions. Sprinkle flour out on the surface where you are going to roll dough. Sprinkle flour on top of dough and on rolling pin. Roll out to desired size and place in pie or flan dish. Trim or flute edges. Fork sides and bottom.

3. Now this step is called baking the case 'blind'. Line each case with greaseproof paper or foil and cover with ceramic baking beads. Place in a preheated oven 190C/375F/gas mark 5 for 15 minutes. Take out of oven, remove baking beads and liner. Brush each case with beaten egg and put back in oven for another 15 minutes.

MARY'S TIP

*If you do not have ceramic baking beads, use any dried beans or macaroni.*

# SHEPHERD'S PIE

A simple dish that will have your family members begging for more.

SERVES 6

MINUTES 90

DIFFICULTY 5/10

## INGREDIENTS

### FILLING

**3 tbsp vegetable oil**

**2 medium onions, chopped**

**2 beef stock cubes**

**450ml (15fl oz) boiling water**

**450g (1lb) lean ground beef (minced beef)**

**3 carrots, peeled and finely diced**

**1 tbsp dried mixed herbs**

**2 garlic cloves, finely chopped**

**1 tbsp Dijon mustard**

**sea salt and freshly ground pepper to taste**

### TOPPING

**8 medium potatoes, peeled and chopped**

**50g (2oz) butter (grass-fed if possible)**

**75ml (3fl oz) milk**

**110g (4oz) cheddar, grated**

## METHOD

### FILLING

1. Heat the oil and soften the onions.
2. Add the stock cubes to boiling water and set aside.
3. Add the beef to the onions and gently brown. Add the carrots, mixed herbs, garlic, Dijon mustard, salt and pepper.
4. Now add the beef stock and bring to a gentle boil, and then simmer gently for one hour to reduce.
5. Spoon into a casserole dish and allow to cool.

### TOPPING

1. Chop the potatoes and boil in salted water until soft.
2. Once soft, drain and then mash potato, and add the butter, milk and season to taste, blend until creamy.
3. Preheat the oven to 180C/350F/gas mark 4.
4. Spoon the potato mixture gently on top of the meat in equal amounts so that the potato completely seals the beef once you gently fork it over.
5. Sprinkle grated cheddar on top and bake in the oven for 20 minutes.

MARY'S TIP

For a healthier option – you can replace the lean ground (minced) beef with lean ground (minced) turkey and the potato with sweet potato.

# PORK AVENOISE

SERVES
4

MINUTES
20

DIFFICULTY
2/10

A quick and easy super-tasty supper – a family and friends impresser. This is a two-part process.

## INGREDIENTS

**12 medallions of pork fillet (cut 2cm [0.75"] thick from a pork loin)**

**2 tbsp sunflower oil**

**240ml (8fl oz) white wine**

**1 chicken or ham stock cube**

**1 tbsp Dijon mustard**

**1 heaped tsp red chilli flakes**

**175g (6oz) grated mature cheddar**

**300ml (10fl oz) double cream**

**1 tsp cracked black pepper**

**sprinkle of paprika**

## METHOD

1 Heat a frying pan and gently fry the medallions in the sunflower oil until nicely browned on one side. Turn and continue cooking until browned and cooked through, then remove from pan and put to one side.

2 Pour the wine into the frying pan, add the stock cube and gently bring to a boil whisking continually. Turn down the heat to a brisk simmer.

3 Add the Dijon mustard and chilli flakes and continue to whisk for a few minutes. Add the mature cheddar cheese and continue to stir the sauce until it resembles a paste, at this point add the cream and black pepper. Bring to the boil and then quickly turn down to a simmer. Allow to simmer for 10 minutes and continue to stir at intervals.

4 Place the pork medallions in the sauce and simmer for a further five minutes. Serve topped with a sprinkle of paprika.

## MARY'S TIP

If you find sauce is too thick, add liquid stock or white wine to desired consistency.

# LUXURY FISH PIE

This fish pie is a family favourite – don't hesitate adding prawns, mussels or hot smoked salmon.

SERVES
6

MINUTES
60

DIFFICULTY
4/10

## INGREDIENTS

### FILLING

**900g (2lb) smoked haddock fillets (450g/1lb dyed and 450g/1lb undyed)**

**900ml (30fl oz) milk**

**110g (4oz) butter**

**3 hard-boiled eggs, roughly chopped**

**3 tbsp fresh parsley**

**2 tbsp capers**

**juice and grated rind of 1 lemon**

**60g (2.5oz) flour**

**sea salt and freshly milled black pepper**

### TOPPING

**900g (2lb) boiled potatoes**

**50g (2oz) butter**

**4 tbsp milk**

**50g (2oz) mature cheddar cheese, grated**

## METHOD

### FILLING

1 Preheat the oven to 180C/350F/gas mark 4.

2 Arrange the haddock in a baking dish, pour half of the milk over the fish and add 50g (2oz) of butter. Bake in the oven for 20 minutes. Pour off the excess liquid and reserve, then flake the fish into large pieces and layer the chopped eggs, parsley, capers, lemon juice and rind with fish.

3 Melt the remaining butter in a saucepan. Add the flour to form a roux then slowly add the reserved liquid stirring continually. Add the remaining milk, continue to stir. Season and simmer for 4 minutes then pour mixture on top of fish and mix.

### TOPPING

1 Mash the potatoes into a nice creamy consistency, for a really creamy mash use a potato ricer. Season and then add the butter and milk. Spread the mashed potato evenly over the fish and finish off with a sprinkle of cheese.

2 Bake in the oven for around 30 minutes.

MARY'S TIP

You can use sweet potato if you prefer – also I sometimes mix some chopped spring onions through the mashed potato.

# HOT CHILLI CON CARNE

SERVES
10-12

MINUTES
120

DIFFICULTY
3/10

This great chilli recipe has to be one of the best dishes to serve to friends for a casual get-together or party.

## INGREDIENTS

**2 tbsp olive oil**

**2 large Spanish onions, chopped**

**900g (2lb) lean ground beef (minced beef)**

**6 garlic cloves, chopped**

**1 tube tomato paste**

**2 red chillies, chopped with seeds included**

**2 green chillies, chopped with seeds included**

**1.5 tbsp ground cumin**

**2 tbsp chilli powder**

**2 heaped tbsp of dried mixed herbs**

**200ml (7fl oz) red wine**

**4 x 400g tins chopped tomatoes**

**3 x 400g tins kidney beans**

**seasoning to taste**

## METHOD

1 Heat the oil in large pot, add the onions and sauté slowly.

2 Add the beef and gently brown.

3 Next add the garlic and tomato paste mixing well, cook for 1 minute.

4 Add the chillies, cumin, chilli powder and mixed herbs. Stir well.

5 Add the red wine and simmer for 2 minutes, add the chopped tomatoes, kidney beans and season to taste. Cook on a low heat for 1.5 hrs.

## MARY'S TIP

Serve with rice or make a chilli wrap by placing the chilli in the middle of a large tortilla wrap, fold sides onto top of chilli and then top with grated cheese and place under grill until cheese bubbles. Now top with a dollop of crème fraîche, slices of red onion and some sliced jalapeños.

# SMOKED HADDOCK KEDGEREE

SERVES
4

MINUTES
40

DIFFICULTY
5/10

A great Sunday brunch favourite!

## INGREDIENTS

**600ml (20fl oz) boiling water**

**450g (1lb) undyed smoked haddock fillet**

**2 tbsp olive oil**

**1 large onion, finely chopped**

**2 cloves garlic, finely chopped**

**1 tsp turmeric**

**1 tsp ground cumin**

**2 tsp ground coriander**

**225g (8oz) long grain rice**

**1 bunch of spring onions, finely chopped**

**3 tbsp butter**

**1 tbsp fresh parsley, chopped**

**1 tbsp fresh coriander, chopped**

**4 eggs, hard boiled**

**lemon wedges to garnish**

## METHOD

1 Pour the boiling water over the haddock and leave for 10 minutes.

2 Lift the fish from the cooking water and flake (discard any bones or skin) reserving the fish stock.

3 Heat the oil in large saucepan and add the onion. Cook over a medium heat for 10 minutes.

4 Add the garlic, turmeric, cumin and coriander and stir for 1 minute. Add the rice and stir well.

5 Measure 475ml (16fl oz) of the fish stock and add to saucepan. Stir well and bring to boil. Cover and cook over a very low heat for 12-15 minutes until the rice is tender and water absorbed.

6 Add the haddock, butter, spring onions and fresh herbs, stirring well. Cook for 2 minutes or until butter melts.

7 Shell and quarter the hard-boiled eggs and arrange them around your serving plate along with lemon wedges.

MARY'S TIP

Sprinkle with chopped chives. You can also swap the smoked haddock for hot smoked salmon for a different flavour.

# FISH CAKES

SERVES
6-8

MINUTES
180

DIFFICULTY
5/10

Good old-fashioned fish cakes that will have you coming back for seconds, serve them with a simple tomato salsa for a tasty supper.

## INGREDIENTS

**8 large potatoes, peeled**

**6 smoked haddock fillets (3 dyed and 3 undyed)**

**50g (2oz) butter (grass-fed if possible)**

**300ml (10fl oz) milk**

**sea salt and freshly ground black pepper**

**1 bunch of spring onions, finely chopped**

**2 tsp fresh dill, chopped**

**juice from one lemon**

**2 tsp fish seasoning**

**1 tbsp capers**

**225g (8oz) flour**

**4 eggs, beaten**

**225g (8oz) dried breadcrumbs, or 110g (4oz) fresh breadcrumbs, or 175g (6oz) ground cornflakes**

**3 tbsp vegetable oil**

## METHOD

1. Preheat the oven to 190C/375F/gas mark 5.
2. Boil potatoes until soft, then mash.
3. Place fish into a baking dish and cover with butter, milk and freshly ground black pepper. Cover with foil and allow to poach for 20 minutes in the oven or until fish flakes easily.
4. Drain off all liquid from fish. Flake the fish and place in a large bowl with mashed potato, onions, dill, lemon juice, fish seasoning, and capers. With a potato masher blend mixture well ensuring all ingredients are well combined. Allow mixture to cool and then place in refrigerator for 2 hours.
5. Form mixture into 6 or 8 equal sized fish cakes. Coat in flour, dip into beaten egg and then coat in breadcrumbs or cornflakes. Continue until all fish cakes have gone through this process.
6. In a large frying pan heat the vegetable oil. Do not allow the oil to get too hot or the breadcrumbs will burn.
7. Place fish cakes into oil and fry for 3 minutes on each side. Turn out onto paper towel to absorb excess oil.
8. Enjoy with wedges of lemon and tartar sauce.

## MARY'S TIP

Fish cakes can be made ahead of time and then gently reheated in oven for 15 minutes in a moderate heat. They also freeze successfully for up to one month. You can also swap the haddock for salmon and follow the same process.

# HOT MAMA'S SPICY TURKEY MEATLOAF

SERVES
4-6

MINUTES
90

DIFFICULTY
3/10

This is a wonderfully tasty meatloaf and if there are any leftovers (which is doubtful) they make fabulous meatloaf sandwiches.

## INGREDIENTS

**2 tbsp coconut oil**

**1 small onion, chopped**

**2 carrots, peeled and chopped**

**2 celery sticks, chopped**

**3 to 4 garlic cloves, chopped**

**900g (2lb) lean ground turkey (minced turkey)**

**75g (3oz) breadcrumbs**

**1 egg**

**1 red chilli, deseeded and chopped**

**2 tsp paprika**

**2 tbsp fresh sage, chopped**

**sea salt and pepper**

**2 sliced tomatoes to top**

## METHOD

1. Preheat the oven to 180C/350F/gas mark 4.
2. Sauté the onion, carrots, celery and garlic in coconut oil for 20 minutes.
3. Mix the turkey, breadcrumbs, egg, chilli, paprika and sage in a large bowl and add the sautéed vegetables mixing well. Season and turn out into a loaf tin.
4. Top with tomatoes then bake in the oven for 1 hour 10 minutes.

MARY'S TIP

Makes an excellent accompaniment to any picnic – great served cold as well as hot.

# COCONUT PRAWNS

SERVES
4

MINUTES
30

DIFFICULTY
2/10

This is a prawn dish that is just bursting with ethnic Asian flavours.

## INGREDIENTS

**1 tbsp coconut oil**

**4 spring onions, chopped**

**1 small onion, diagonally sliced**

**2.5cm (1") ginger, chopped**

**3 garlic cloves, chopped**

**1 red chilli, chopped**

**1 green chilli, chopped**

**1 stalk lemongrass, chopped**

**1.5 tbsp curry powder**

**1 tsp turmeric**

**240ml (8fl oz) coconut milk**

**450g (1lb) raw king prawns**

**1 small red and orange sweet peppers, sliced**

**handful of either mange tout or green beans, chopped**

**2 tbsp fresh coriander, chopped**

**juice and rind of one lime**

## METHOD

1. Heat the coconut oil on a medium heat then add the onions, ginger, garlic, chillies and lemongrass, and sauté gently for 3 minutes.
2. Add the spices and coconut milk and cook for a further 5 mins.
3. Next add the prawns, peppers and mange tout and bring to a gentle boil for 2 minutes.
4. Turn heat off and add lime and coriander. Leave for 5 minutes.

MARY'S TIP

Serve with either white basmati, brown rice or quinoa.

# CHICKEN & SPINACH CURRY

SERVES
6

MINUTES
80

DIFFICULTY
5/10

This dish can be prepared the day before to infuse flavours but only add spinach when you're getting ready to serve to keep its green vibrancy.

## INGREDIENTS

**2 tbsp coconut oil**

**1 large onion, chopped**

**1 tbsp fresh ginger, chopped**

**4 or 5 garlic cloves, peeled and chopped**

**3 chicken breasts, cubed**

**2 red chillies, finely chopped**

**1 green chilli, finely chopped**

**1 tbsp ground coriander**

**1 tbsp ground cumin**

**1 tsp turmeric**

**sea salt and pepper**

**2 large tbsp Greek yoghurt**

**1 x 400g tin coconut milk**

**2 tomatoes, chopped**

**1 handful fresh coriander (cilantro), chopped**

**3 handfuls baby leaf spinach**

## METHOD

1. Heat the coconut oil and add the onion, ginger and garlic. Sauté gently over a low heat.
2. Add the chicken turning frequently to ensure the chicken cooks on all sides.
3. Add the chopped chillies, spices, sea salt and pepper stirring well.
4. Add the yoghurt and then coconut milk. Stir and add the freshly chopped tomatoes.
5. Bring to the boil then turn quickly down to a simmer for 60 minutes.
6. Add freshly chopped coriander (cilantro) and the spinach and cook for a further 15 minutes on a low heat.

## MARY'S TIP

Add some fresh mango – say 75g (3oz) and/or 25g (1oz) shredded coconut. Serve with basmati rice or any other long grain or wholegrain rice along with naan bread or chapatis.

# STEAK & ALE PIE

SERVES
4

MINUTES
120

DIFFICULTY
5/10

A hearty favourite winter warmer – nothing is nicer than tucking into some melt-in-the-mouth Aberdeen Angus and a crispy puff pastry topping.

## INGREDIENTS

**2 tbsp olive oil**

**2 medium onions, chopped**

**3 garlic cloves, chopped**

**4 tbsp of plain flour seasoned with salt and pepper**

**450g (1lb) cubed Aberdeen Angus steak**

**475ml (16fl oz) beef stock**

**240ml (8fl oz) dark traditional Scottish ale**

**1 tbsp tomato paste**

**3 medium carrots, diced**

**1 pack of ready-made puff pastry**

**1 egg, beaten**

## METHOD

1 Sauté the chopped onions and garlic in the olive oil.

2 To a bowl add the seasoned flour (this will help thicken the sauce later) coat the steak and add to the pan in batches, browning gently.

3 Add the stock, ale, tomato paste and diced carrots. Bring to the boil, then cover the pan, turn the heat down to a gentle simmer and allow to cook for 1.5 hours. Gently stir and check every 15-20 minutes.

4 Transfer to an ovenproof dish and allow to cool a little.

5 Preheat the oven to 180C/350F/gas mark 4.

6 Cut the puff pastry to the shape of your dish allowing for a small overlap. Cut a small cross in centre of pastry to allow steam to escape.

7 Place the pastry over top of your meat dish. Brush with beaten egg. Bake in preheated oven for 15 minutes. Do not open oven or pastry will fall.

MARY'S TIP

You can use any type of cubed beef steak.

# CHICKEN BALTI WITH CHERRY TOMATOES & FLAKED ALMONDS

SERVES
4

MINUTES
20

DIFFICULTY
2/10

Baltis are basically Indian stir fry. Making your own balti paste is well worth the effort – see recipe on page 92.

## INGREDIENTS

**4 tbsp coconut oil**

**6 tbsp toasted flaked almonds**

**4 skinless chicken breasts, cubed**

**2 onions, finely chopped**

**6 tbsp balti paste (see page 92)**

**2 tbsp coriander leaves, freshly chopped**

**16 cherry tomatoes, halved**

## METHOD

1. Heat 1 tbsp of coconut oil in large pan or wok and quickly fry the almonds until they start to colour, remove from the pan and put aside.
2. Add the remaining coconut oil to the pan and cook the chicken breasts over a high heat for 5 minutes until lightly browned all over. Remove from pan.
3. Add the onion to the pan and cook until golden.
4. Return the chicken to the pan, stir in the balti paste, coriander leaves and tomatoes. Stir over a medium heat for 10 minutes.
5. Garnish with the fried almonds.

### MARY'S TIP

This is excellent served with butter rice or plain basmati rice, naan bread or chapatis along with a selection of chutneys.

# PRAWN BALTI CURRY

SERVES
4

MINUTES
20

DIFFICULTY
3/10

This has a mild, creamy taste with the addition of Greek or natural yoghurt.

## INGREDIENTS

**2 tbsp coconut oil**

**1 medium onion, finely chopped**

**450g (1lb) large raw shelled prawns (you can substitute frozen peeled prawns, but make sure they are thoroughly defrosted before use)**

**3 tbsp balti paste (see recipe on page 92)**

**1 red pepper, deseeded and chopped into chunks**

**1 green pepper, deseeded and chopped into chunks**

**1 x 400g tin chopped tomatoes**

**75ml (3fl oz) natural Greek yoghurt**

**2 tbsp fresh coriander leaves, chopped**

**lemon wedges to garnish**

## METHOD

1. Heat the coconut oil in large pan or wok. Add the onion and cook over a medium heat until golden.
2. Add the prawns and the balti paste and mix, and cook together for about 2 minutes until the prawns are evenly coated and turning pink.
3. Stir in peppers, tomatoes and yoghurt, and cook for a further 5 minutes.
4. Add coriander leaves and serve. Garnish with lemon wedges and serve with saffron, butter or basmati rice.

### MARY'S TIP

This dish can be altered to make a fish balti by replacing prawns with 450g (1lb) of cod or any other white fish. I choose cod as it flakes into big pieces.

# BALTI PASTE

SERVES 12

MINUTES 20

DIFFICULTY 3/10

This is a great paste to make up as it will keep in an airtight container in the fridge for up to 2 weeks, or frozen for up to a month, a truly authentic-tasting balti.

## INGREDIENTS

**4 tbsp coconut oil, or ghee**

**2 red chillies, finely chopped (if you prefer a milder paste, deseed chillies)**

**3 medium onions, finely chopped**

**2 tsp fresh ginger, grated**

**6 garlic cloves, peeled and chopped**

**1 tsp ground turmeric**

**3 tbsp ground coriander**

**1.5 tsp ground cumin**

**5 packs fresh coriander, chopped**

**1 x 227g tin chopped tomatoes**

**1.5 tsp sea salt**

**1 tsp coconut sugar**

**2 tsp garam masala**

## METHOD

1. Heat the oil in a heavy frying pan and add the chillies. When they start to crackle, add the onion and cook over a medium heat until the onion is soft and transparent.
2. Add the ginger, garlic, turmeric, ground coriander, cumin and half the coriander leaves. Stir over the heat for 4 minutes.
3. Add the tomatoes, sea salt, sugar and garam masala and 120ml (4fl oz) water. Cover and cook over a medium heat for 10 minutes.
4. Remove from the heat and stir in the remaining coriander leaves.

## MARY'S TIP

If you have a hand-held processor, put chillies into the small tub with blade as this chops chillies perfectly for this paste. This paste can be used for the Chicken Balti and Chicken and Spinach Curry recipes – for spicy food lovers, these are dynamite.

# BUTTER RICE

SERVES
4

MINUTES
85

DIFFICULTY
1/10

This luxurious rice dish can be served with any type of curry.

## INGREDIENTS

**225g (8oz) long grain rice**

**50g (2oz) butter**

**1 garlic clove, peeled and chopped**

**475ml (16fl oz) vegetable or chicken stock**

**2 tbsp fresh parsley, chopped**

**110g (4oz) toasted flaked almonds**

## METHOD

1. Soak the rice for 30 minutes in boiling water and rinse well.
2. Preheat the oven to 180C/350F/gas mark 4.
3. Melt the butter in a frying pan then add the rice and cook for 10 minutes until butter is well absorbed.
4. Add the garlic and then put the rice into a 900ml (40fl oz) casserole dish.
5. Add the stock of your choice then stir. Place a lid on the casserole dish and put in oven. Cook for 45 minutes.
6. Finish off by adding parsley and mix through rice. Replace lid and leave for 10 minutes before serving.
7. Top with toasted almonds.

MARY'S TIP

Make sure the rice absorbs all the butter.

# DESSERTS

# AWARD-WINNING PAVLOVA

SERVES
6

MINUTES
90

DIFFICULTY
6/10

For a great pavlova you want to achieve a crispy outer shell and fluffy moist meringue inside. I have 2 secrets to share.

## INGREDIENTS

### MERINGUE

**6 egg whites**
*(chill eggs for at least a couple of days before use - SECRET NO. 1)*

**225g (8oz) caster sugar**
*(grind sugar in a mini blender until like icing sugar - SECRET NO. 2)*

**1 tsp cornflour**

**1 tsp malt vinegar**

**0.5 tsp vanilla essence**

### TOPPING

**300ml (10fl oz) double cream**

**your favourite fruit (strawberries, mandarins, passion fruit)**

## METHOD

### MERINGUE

1 Beat the egg whites until you obtain fluffy self-holding peaks. Slowly beat in the sugar then beat in the remainder of the ingredients.

2 Put greaseproof paper on a baking sheet. Pour the meringue mixture onto the paper to form a circle and make a slight well in centre.

3 Bake for 30 minutes at 150C, 300F, gas mark 2, then turn oven down to 140C, 275F, gas mark 1 and bake for a further 30 minutes, turn down oven again to 120C, 250F, gas mark 0.5 and bake for a further 30 minutes. Turn oven off and allow pavlova to totally cool inside the oven. Do not worry if shell cracks or middle drops as this is going to be covered in a fruit of your choice and whipped cream.

### TOPPING

1 Whip the double cream. Pour this into the centre of the meringue. Decorate with your favourite fruit.

MARY'S TIP

This is best left in the oven overnight to cool slowly.

# LEMON & LIME CHEESECAKE

SERVES
6-8

MINUTES
240

DIFFICULTY
2/10

An enormous favourite when I had my restaurant. It was the dessert that sparked off my first book when I owned my bistro and gallery.

## INGREDIENTS

### BASE

**20cm (8") round, spring-form tin with deep sides**

**225g (8oz) digestive biscuits, crushed**

**50g (2oz) ginger biscuits, crushed**

**175g (6oz) butter, melted**

### FILLING

**225g (8oz) cream cheese**

**300ml (10fl oz) double cream**

**1 x 400g tin condensed milk**

**juice of one lemon and two limes**

**grated rind of one lemon and two limes**

## METHOD

### BASE

1. Mix together crushed biscuits and butter. You want the biscuit crumbs to be well coated in butter to ensure they press firmly into the pie dish.
2. Press mixture onto the base and sides of the tin. Refrigerate for one hour before use.

### FILLING

1. Blend the cream cheese and double cream in a large mixing bowl with a hand mixer. Add the condensed milk to this mixture and blend well.
2. Add the juice of the lemon, lime and grated rind. (Save a little grated rind to sprinkle on top of cheesecake.) Mix on high speed until the mixture thickens slightly.
3. Pour into the prepared base and sprinkle with the grated rind.
4. Allow to set for 3 hours in the fridge.

MARY'S TIP

Serve with freshly whipped cream on the side and some fresh lemon and lime slices.

# CRANACHAN

SERVES
4

MINUTES
30

DIFFICULTY
1/10

This is a traditional Scottish dessert using two of Scotland's staple products – oatmeal and whisky.

## INGREDIENTS

**6 to 8 tbsp oatmeal**

**600ml (20fl oz) double cream**

**4 tbsp good quality honey**

**4 tbsp single malt whisky**

**425g (15oz) raspberries**

## METHOD

1. Place the oatmeal in a cool dry pan and toast on a medium heat. Stir occasionally until golden brown, this could take 10-15 minutes.
2. Once the oatmeal is brown, take the pan off the heat and leave to cool.
3. Place the cream in a bowl and whisk up until thick. Add the honey and single malt whisky and fold into the cream using a whisk.
4. Arrange four raspberries in the bottom of each serving glass. Now layer with cream and a sprinkle of toasted oatmeal and continue with layers.
5. Top off each one with a sprinkling of oatmeal and decorate with a raspberry.
6. Chill for 3 hours or overnight.

MARY'S TIP

You can also skip the toasted oatmeal step and use a luxury quality granola.

# STICKY GINGERBREAD

MAKES 4 X 450G (1LB) LOAVES

MINUTES 55

DIFFICULTY 3/10

A great afternoon teatime addition.

You will need 4 x 450g (1lb) loaf tins, I like to use the greaseproof loaf liners – much easier and no need to oil them. Divide ingredients in half to make smaller quantities.

## INGREDIENTS

**225g (8oz) butter**

**225g (8oz) soft dark brown sugar**

**225g (8oz) black treacle or molasses**

**350g (12oz) plain flour**

**2 tsp ground ginger**

**1 tbsp ground cinnamon**

**2 tsp bicarbonate of soda**

**2 eggs, beaten**

**300ml (10fl oz) milk**

## METHOD

1. Preheat the oven to 150C/300F/gas mark 2. Prepare loaf tins either by brushing lightly with oil or placing one greaseproof liner in each tin.
2. Melt the butter, sugar and treacle together in a saucepan. Tip the mixture into a large bowl and allow to cool to room temperature.
3. Sift the flour, ginger, cinnamon and bicarbonate of soda into a separate bowl and make a well in the centre.
4. Stir the beaten eggs and milk into the butter mixture. Tip the butter mixture into the well in the flour and fold in quickly with a large metal spoon and whisk. Pour equally into your prepared loaf tins.
5. Place in the middle of the oven and bake for 35 minutes or until loaves are well risen and spring back on touch. Place on wire rack to cool.
6. Wrap in foil and store in a cool dry place for up to 5 days or freeze for up to one month.

MARY'S TIP

I like to use the greaseproof loaf liners in my loaf tins.

# PECAN PIE

Pecan nuts are a favourite in the U.S.A. where they are used extensively in baking as well as being eaten as a dessert nut. Try making with walnuts or hazelnuts.

You will need a cooked 20cm (8") sweet pastry shell made in a loose-bottomed flan tin, see page 66 for pastry recipe.

## INGREDIENTS

**110g (4oz) soft brown sugar**

**50g (2oz) maple syrup**

**150g (5oz) golden syrup**

**3 eggs, beaten**

**60g (2.5oz) butter, melted**

**1 tsp vanilla essence**

**175-225g (6-8oz) pecans**

**set aside 75g (3oz) of the pecans for decorating the top of the pie**

## METHOD

1 Place all the ingredients in a food processor and blend until the nuts are coarsely chopped.

2 Pour the mixture into the cooked pastry case.

3 Arrange the remaining pecan halves on top of the pie in a circular pattern around the edge.

4 Preheat the oven to 180C/350F/gas mark 4. Bake the pie towards the top of the oven for about 30 minutes or until filling is firm to touch.

MARY'S TIP

Delicious served warm with a scoop of vanilla ice-cream or fresh whipped cream.

# LEMON TART

A simple yet great finisher to any meal, it has a tangy lemony tartness that zings one's taste buds.

You will need a cooked 20cm (8") fluted pastry case, for recipe see page 66.

## INGREDIENTS

**5 eggs**

**200g (7oz) caster sugar**

**rind of 3 lemons, finely grated**

**110g (4oz) unsalted butter, melted**

**juice of 3 lemons**

**juice of 1 orange**

## METHOD

1. Preheat the oven to 180C/350F/gas mark 4.
2. Place the eggs, sugar and lemon rind into a food processor. Blend until well mixed.
3. Add the melted butter whilst the processor is still running then add the juice of the lemons and orange. Blend for 30 seconds so mixture does not get too frothy.
4. Pour the filling into the prepared pastry case and bake for 25-30 minutes or until firm to touch.

MARY'S TIP

*Just before serving, lightly dust with icing sugar.*

# STICKY TOFFEE PUDDING & CARAMEL SAUCE

MINUTES
60

DIFFICULTY
3/10

This pudding lends itself well to being heated up first before serving.

## INGREDIENTS

### PUDDING

**50g (2oz) unsalted butter, softened**

**150g (5oz) caster sugar**

**1 egg, beaten**

**200g (7oz) self-raising flour**

**1 tsp baking powder**

**175g (6oz) dates, chopped**

**1 tsp bicarbonate soda**

**300ml (10fl oz) boiling water**

### SAUCE

**275g (10oz) brown sugar**

**300ml (10fl oz) double cream**

**275g (10oz) unsalted butter**

## METHOD

### PUDDING

1 Cream the butter and sugar together. Add the egg and beat well. Stir in flour and baking powder. Put the dates and bicarbonate of soda in a bowl and pour over the boiling water. Mix thoroughly into the creamed mixture.

2 Grease a deep baking dish (30 x 20 x 13cm [12 x 8 x 5"]) and sprinkle the bottom with a little caster sugar. Pour the pudding mixture into the dish.

3 Preheat the oven to 180C/350F/gas mark 4 and bake for 35-40 minutes.

### SAUCE

1 Put the brown sugar, cream and butter in a pan, bring to boil and simmer until the sauce turns a caramel colour. Pour the warm caramel sauce over the pudding to serve.

## MARY'S TIP

Vanilla ice-cream on the side is a must.

# BANOFFI PIE

SERVES
6

MINUTES
60

DIFFICULTY
3/10

This pie is a mixture of bananas, toffee and cream and will always put smiles on the faces of those you are serving it to.

*You will need a 20cm (8") spring-form cake tin.*

## INGREDIENTS

### BASE

**225g (8oz) digestive biscuits, crushed**

**50g (2oz) ginger biscuits, crushed**

**175g (6oz) butter, melted**

### FILLING

**175g (6oz) butter**

**75g (3oz) caster sugar**

**75g (3oz) dark brown sugar**

**2 x 400g tins condensed milk**

**4 bananas**

**450ml (15fl oz) double cream**

**1 chocolate flake or cocoa powder for dusting**

## METHOD

### BASE

1 Mix together crushed biscuits and butter. You want the biscuit crumbs to be well coated in butter to ensure they press firmly into the pie dish.

2 Press mixture onto the base and sides of a 20cm (8") pie dish. Refrigerate for one hour before use.

### FILLING

1 Place butter and the sugars in a non-stick saucepan over a low heat, stirring until butter melts and sugars are dissolved.

2 Add the condensed milk and bring to a gentle boil, stirring continuously. Boil steadily for exactly 2 minutes, stirring frequently, to make a golden caramel.

3 Spread caramel over biscuit base and chill for 1 to 2 hours or until firm.

4 To serve, slice bananas thinly and arrange most of them over the caramel.

5 With a hand mixer whip the double cream, then spread it over the bananas. Decorate with remaining bananas, crumbled chocolate flake or cocoa powder.

MARY'S TIP

Once you cut up bananas to decorate top – coat them in lemon juice to prevent them going brown.

# SCONES (PLAIN OR FRUIT)

UTES
25

DIFFICULTY
2/10

Scones are a traditional British pastry that are simple and easy to make. A must component for an authentic British cream tea.

## INGREDIENTS

**700g (1lb 9oz) self-raising flour**

**2 tsp baking powder**

**175g (6oz) butter or margarine, softened**

**75g (3oz) caster sugar**

**350ml (12fl oz) milk**

**1 tsp vanilla extract**

**110g (4oz) raisins, sultanas or currants**

## METHOD

1. Sift flour and baking powder into large bowl. Rub the butter into flour until it is like fine breadcrumbs.
2. Stir in the sugar (at this point if you want a fruit scone, add your dried fruit of choice). Gently warm the milk in a pan and add the vanilla.
3. Make a well in the dry ingredients and add milk. Fold the flour into milk quickly. It may seem sticky at first but keep folding the dough over a few times.
4. Turn out onto a floured surface and sprinkle with flour. Pat dough to 4cm (1.5") deep and using a cutter, cut out the scones.
5. Glaze the tops with milk and place on a hot baking tray.
6. Preheat the oven to 200C/400F/gas mark 6. Bake for around 15 mins or until risen and golden.